DAYS
OF
HOPE
AND
DREAMS

AN
INTIMATE
PORTRAIT
OF
BRUCE
SPRINGSTEEN

This book is published in conjunction with the exhibition
DAYS OF HOPE AND DREAMS:
PHOTOGRAPHS BY FRANK STEFANKO
at GOVINDA GALLERY
1227 Thirty-fourth Street N.W.
Washington, D.C. 20007
www.govindagallery.com

BILLBOARD BOOKS
an imprint of Watson-Guptill Publications/New York

Produced by Watson-Guptill Publications and
INSIGHT EDITIONS
1299 4th St., Suite 305, San Rafael, CA 94901
www.insighteditions.com

First published in 2003 by Billboard Books,
an imprint of Watson-Guptill Publications,
a division of VNU Business Media, Inc.,
770 Broadway, New York, N.Y. 10003
www.watsonguptill.com

Library of Congress Cataloging-in-Publication Data is on file
with the Library of Congress.
Library of Congress Control Number: 2003106291
ISBN: 0-8230-8387-X

Edited by Chris Murray
Executive Editor: Bob Nirkind
Project Editor: Elizabeth Wright
Cover design and interior by Spencer Drate and Judith Salavetz

Printed in China by Palace Press International
www.palacepress.com
First printing, 2003
1 2 3 4 5 6 7 8 9 / 09 08 07 06 05 04 03

DAYS OF HOPE AND DREAMS

AN
INTIMATE
PORTRAIT
OF
BRUCE
SPRINGSTEEN

BILLBOARD BOOKS
AN IMPRINT OF
WATSON-GUPTILL PUBLICATIONS
NEW YORK

A Star Shines in the Sky

Sheila Ruth Stefanko 1944-1985

CONTENTS

Foreword by Chris Murray   6

Preface by Frank Stefanko   8

Introduction by Bruce Springsteen   10

BEGINNINGS   12

HADDONFIELD, NEW JERSEY, 1978   18

EAST CAMDEN, NEW JERSEY, 1978   40

NEW YORK CITY, NEW YORK, 1978   50

PHILADELPHIA, PENNSYLVANIA, 1978–
NEW YORK CITY, NEW YORK, 1980   72

HADDONFIELD, NEW JERSEY, 1982   86

MONMOUTH COUNTY, NEW JERSEY, 1982   110

Afterword   133

Acknowledgments   135

FOREWORD

Over the past thirty years, Bruce Springsteen has established himself as an icon of American songwriting and as a performer of legendary proportions. Springsteen's cast of characters and their search for redemption describe a way of life that is central to the experiences of many of us. His musical journey has taken us down long stretches of the road we all travel. In fact, his artistry has become a part of the great American cultural landscape.

Frank Stefanko's photographs of Bruce Springsteen, taken between 1978 and 1982, provide an extraordinary portrait of the artist at a crucial time in his life and career. Stefanko's images on the covers of *Darkness on the Edge of Town* and *The River*, Springsteen's acclaimed recordings from this period, are classics. These photographs realize the moment. They are not just of Bruce Springsteen—they are *about* Bruce Springsteen.

The Haddonfield, New Jersey pictures taken in 1978 are among the best photographs of Springsteen. These images of him standing outside a barbershop, leaning on his Corvette, or simply relaxing at the photographer's home evoke a mood of expectation, of extraordinary things to come. In photos of Springsteen with the E Street Band at Shellow's Luncheonette in East Camden, the sense of easy camaraderie among these kindred spirits is apparent.

The rooftop photographs taken in New York City that same year parallel earlier images of rock and roll's progenitor, Elvis Presley. Springsteen's connection to the sources that inspire him—the rich American legacy of rock and roll and rhythm and blues—is evident in these photos. The classic portraits of Springsteen with his acoustic guitar are visual evidence of his interest in country music. Like that of Hank Williams, Springsteen's work defines the quintessential American spirit.

Springsteen's music has entered the American vernacular. His search for and experience of transcendence fills his songs with significance. Frank Stefanko's photographs, like Bruce Springsteen's songs, won't fade away.

Chris Murray
Director, Govinda Gallery

PREFACE

Somewhere back in the early fifties, about the time Elvis Presley was still driving a truck for a living, I found an old box camera that belonged to my father. I asked him if I could mess around with it. He said I could have it, and gave me a couple rolls of 120 film and showed me how to load them. I was eight years old, it was 1954, and Katie, bar the door—I was hooked. I became an eight-year-old photo junkie; I couldn't get enough.

I had an abundance of art training in those days: It was called "TV." I loved to watch old movies—all those great black-and-white film noir mysteries, Saturday morning Westerns, pretty much whatever they threw up on that screen, I was taking it all in. I couldn't have had better art teachers. I knew about composition, repetition of shape, subject placement, and tone. It was all there. Guys like James Wong Howe, John Houston, and Fritz Lang taught me, and they didn't even know it.

As the mid- to late fifties rolled in, Elvis rolled out for the world to see. The kids in my town were wearing white T-shirts and blue dungarees, trying to be Elvis or James Dean with the obligatory pack of Camels rolled up in their sleeves. "Blue Moon of Kentucky" begat "Rock Around the Clock" and "Summertime Blues." I had moved up to a Kodak Brownie camera by then and was a hopeless romantic. I was listening to rock and roll, taking photographs, and dreaming about that "Special Angel" and wondering who she would be.

The thing that sealed my fate with photography was a short-lived TV series called *Man with a Camera* starring Charles Bronson as hard-hitting photographer Mike Kovac. Each show, for me, was a religious experience. The only thing that comes close these days are the Alex Rutledge novels by Tom Corcoran. As I grew more adept at my craft, my dad bought me a thirty-five-dollar Federal enlarger out of his hundred-dollar-a-week paycheck, and I felt like the big "E" must have felt when he bought his first Cadillac.

As the fifties evolved into the sixties, music was changing. Motown, surf music, the British invasion, folk, folk rock, acid rock, blues, and, of course, Elvis were all out there, all going around in my head. In a changing world, the one constant for me was photography. The thrill of composing a photograph, from snapping the picture through the entire darkroom process, was a joy I would never lose.

I moved up to a Besseler enlarger and was printing on Agfa Portriga Rapid paper, using Kodak Selectol developer to get warm, deep tones. I had taken fine art classes in high school as well as both art and photography courses in college. On weekends, I went to Manhattan and gave my photographs away at the Chelsea Hotel to get people to recognize my work. Stieglitz, Steichen, Sander, and Arbus were the photographers whose genius added new dimensions to the way I saw things.

I ran around to rock concerts taking photographs of Janis Joplin, Frank Zappa, Rod Stewart & the Faces, the Stones, and pretty much whomever else struck my fancy. Patti Smith was a friend from my college days and my favorite photographic subject back then. Patti had this jet-black hair and pale blue eyes that could see right through you. After we left college, Patti moved to Manhattan. When I visited New York, I started photographing Patti. I was captivated by her look . . . tall, thin, with porcelain skin, sharp features, and those piercing eyes. With me, in terms of portraits, it's always the eyes first, then the rest of the face comes into view.

The mid-seventies were soon upon us, and by then I had a wife and two sons. Elvis was playing Vegas, and I was shooting photographs with my new Mamiya RB 67 camera. Bubble-gum music was sneaking onto the airwaves, and American music was losing direction. That is, until it received a breath of life in the form of Bruce Springsteen. In 1977, Elvis Presley died. In 1978, I was shooting photos of a newly emerging rock and roll icon: Bruce Springsteen.

For me, the period between 1978 and 1982 was more than exciting. I was working with Bruce, who had become my music idol, on the album photography for *Darkness on the Edge of Town* and *The River*. He was making great music. I was creating art, including many of the photographs in this book. Both of us were moving toward something. These were times of growth, magic, and anticipation. For Bruce and myself, they were days of hope and dreams.

Frank Stefanko

INTRODUCTION

In 1977, I was backstage at a Patti Smith concert and she said, "Hey, you ought to have your picture taken by this guy Frank Stefanko." She said he was an old friend who worked in a meatpacking plant in South Jersey and was a really great photographer.

I was on the finishing end of *Darkness on the Edge of Town*, so I gave Frank a call. One winter's day I drove my '60 Vette south to Haddonfield, N.J. We did the session at Frank's house. My recollection is that he borrowed a camera and had the kid next door come over to hold up a big bright light in case where we were shooting grew a little too dark. The cover shot for *Darkness* was taken in Frank's bedroom, and any exterior shots were taken either in Frank's yard or on the streets of Haddonfield.

The pictures were raw. Frank had a way of stripping away any celebrity refuse you may have picked up along the way and finding you in you. He seemed to photograph you within a set of very strict self-imposed limits, but within those limits he created a fully realized world—a world that I felt was deeply connected to the characters I was writing about on *Darkness*. The pictures' lack of grandeur, their directness, their toughness, were what I wanted for my music at that time.

Frank always shot your internal life. He let your external imperfections show. His photos had a purity and poetry; there was some humor in their laconicness. In the aftermath of *Born To Run*, he latched on to the very conflicts and ideas I was struggling to come to terms with: Who am I? Where do I go now? He showed me the people I was writing about in my songs. He showed me the part of me that was still one of them.

Thanks,
Bruce

BEGINNINGS

Bruce's words evoked those moments of being a teenager growing up in New Jersey—or in any small town in America.

I first heard Bruce Springsteen's music on the radio. The FM folk station was broadcasting live from the Main Point coffeehouse in Bryn Mawr, Pennsylvania. One evening, the DJ announced that the featured artist was Bruce Springsteen and the E Street Band. I started listening to this real funky music that had a blistering guitar and tight rhythm section. This guy, Bruce Springsteen, was singing these wild tunes that I really identified with.

Between songs, Bruce told stories about summertime in Freehold, New Jersey, where he was living at the time. Leaning out of his bedroom window, which overlooked Ducky Slattery's Mobil Station, he would watch the guys tuning up their engines while they talked about cars and girlfriends. He talked about the small-town summers spent in white T-shirts and dungarees and being out in Asbury Park, down the shore, or among the Pine Barrens and swamps of New Jersey. Throughout the broadcast, I was thinking, "My God, that's me." Bruce's words evoked those moments of being a teenager growing up in New Jersey, or, for that matter, in any other small town in America. He was hitting those chords, and those familiar feelings were coming through the radio loud and clear. The band sounded so ferocious with that saxophone kicking in and great syncopation. It just sucked me in. All the other music I had been listening to seemed inadequate by comparison; this was so different. It was as if it had been made for *me*. It was the music I had always wanted to hear.

Patti called me up and asked, "Would you like to photograph Bruce Springsteen? He likes the pictures that you did of me."

I kept looking for this band's records, and I told my friend Patti Smith, soon to be a revolutionary musical force in her own right, "Look out for this guy Bruce Springsteen. He's going to be a star someday. He's got a lot of potential." At the time, Patti and I were both students at Glassboro State College (now called Rowan University) in South Jersey. Some time later, after moving to Manhattan, she saw Bruce at a party and told him about this guy in South Jersey who claimed Bruce Springsteen was going to be famous. Patti was starting to become known in Manhattan by giving poetry readings at St. Mark's Church. She was hanging out with William Burroughs, Robert Mapplethorpe, Lou Reed, John Cale, and many other New York artists. New York City was ready for Patti, and Patti was sure ready for the Apple. She was moving up through the New York underground, but it was still a few years before she exploded with her debut album *Horses* in 1975, which featured the Mapplethorpe album cover. A few weeks after mentioning me to Bruce at the party, Patti sent me Bruce's first album, *Greetings From Asbury Park*, and he had written on the back cover: "To Frank, my biggest fan, Patti says. Bruce Springsteen."

Many years later, Patti Smith was at the Record Plant in Manhattan working on an album called *Easter*. Bruce was also there in a different studio working on *Darkness on the Edge of Town*. He was looking at a lot of photography because he didn't have a cover image yet. Apparently, he had seen some pictures that I took of Patti, and he asked her who took them. "It was the same guy that told me about you a long time ago, your South Jersey fan," Patti told him. "Well," Bruce asked, "would he photograph me? Do you think he'd photograph me?" She called me up and asked, "Would you like to photograph Bruce Springsteen? He likes the pictures that you did of me, and he's looking for some new photography, so he's going to give you a call." I immediately told her I was interested.

HADDONFIELD, NEW JERSEY, 1978

Bruce was standing at my door holding a supermarket bag filled with some old denim and plaid shirts, T-shirts, and jeans. That was his wardrobe.

Three months went by, and I had been in and out of New York enough to know that after three months, if nothing had materialized from a conversation about a job, it usually meant you shouldn't expect one. I thought Patti and Bruce's conversation must have just been an example of New York lip service. Then I got a call at home one night, and a vaguely familiar voice said,

"Hey Frank. Let's get together and do some photos."
"Who's this?" I asked.
"Bruce."
"Bruce who?"
"Springsteen, remember? Patti's friend."
"Oh, yeah."

We laughed, and I asked if he wanted me to come up to New York or whether he wanted to come down to Haddonfield, New Jersey, where I was living. Bruce said, "I'll come down." He asked me what he should bring, and I told him to have some changes of clothes so that we could do different sets, different scenes, and whatever else.

A few days later there was a knock at the door. It was winter and there was still snow on the ground. An old white Chevy pick-up truck was parked out front with tree stumps in the back for traction. Bruce was standing at my door holding a supermarket bag filled with some old denim and plaid shirts, T-shirts, and jeans. That was his wardrobe, all crumpled up in a paper grocery bag.

He looked through a lot of pictures and got some idea of what I did. We talked about everything—family, music, photography, art, and life.

At the time, Sheila, my wife and the mother of my children, was still alive. Bruce came in to our house, sat down in the living room, and introduced himself to Sheila and my two sons Keith and Lee. I brought out some of my portfolios of photographs. He looked through a lot of pictures and got some idea of what I did. We talked about everything—family, music, photography, art, and life.

Then we started to take some pictures. I was using a Mamiya RB67, a 6 x 7 centimeter medium format camera. It was my favorite camera. I was also using a two-and-a-quarter twin lens reflex, as well as a 35 millimeter Nikon that I borrowed from a friend. I used several different formats, but the main camera was the RB67 (which, unfortunately, was stolen years ago in New York City).

Bruce would try different poses, or make a couple of suggestions, like turning or leaning against the wall.

I had just moved into the house, so it wasn't completely furnished yet. There were a lot of open nooks and crannies, and we just wandered around. Whenever we saw what looked like a natural environment for a photograph, we lit it up and Bruce would try different poses, or make a couple of suggestions, like turning or leaning against the wall. We just set up little "vignettes," using various angles and different lighting to convey emotions. We shot them off. There was this very strange flowered wallpaper in the house when we bought it. Somebody later called it the most famous wallpaper in the world. Sheila said, "That's my wallpaper. That's our bedroom." We never changed it and it worked very nicely.

We worked the whole day and into the night. When Bruce came back the next day, Sunday, we took some more pictures in and around the house. We would find a step or a corner or some other place, and we just said, let's create a composition within this format. Bruce, like a natural actor, would just fold right into that scene. Like James Dean working his way into a doorway or Clint Eastwood walking down the street, Bruce had a certain way of fitting in, getting himself posed, and knowing what the image should say. We'd try several different versions of a pose, and he would always give it his all.

At the end of a day of shooting we would be exhausted. Both subject and photographer work together building up to that one climax and feeling the rush that comes with snapping that crystal pose. Then the rush subsides, and you have to bring it back up again for the next shot. Boom. Bring it up again. Bruce worked that way tirelessly.

Bruce Springsteen has an unbelievable work ethic. He can work from early morning to late night. For him, it was all about the package, the art. It was all about making it right, and if it wasn't right, he would go back and do it over again until it was. Only then could it be released.

I think Bruce felt pretty safe in Haddonfield. He felt comfortable with my family and me, although we did have a breach in security when Sue Danton, my wife's friend and neighbor, knocked on the door to borrow, of all things, a cup of sugar. We were so impressed with this well-calculated plan to meet Bruce that we invited her in. Bruce gave her a big hug and kiss and laughed as we watched her float down the street, swooning all the way back to her house.

We took walks, just the two of us, out in the streets to take some street shots. People would turn around and say, "Nah, couldn't be. That's not Bruce Springsteen walking down the streets of Haddonfield." They would just shrug it off and walk along. We managed to move through town pretty much unscathed. It was a safe neighborhood.

The shot of Bruce and the barber's pole was taken in front of Frank's Barbershop in Haddonfield. The shop is still there.

People would turn around and say, "Nah, couldn't be. That's not Bruce Springsteen walking down the streets of Haddonfield."

Bruce seemed to come to Haddonfield in a different vehicle each time. After his initial visit in that old Chevy pick-up truck, the next day, Sunday, he arrived in a slick '60 Corvette. I think that car was his pride and joy. It was loaded, it was sleek, it ruled Route 9 and the New Jersey Turnpike. I imagined what it would be like to be Bruce, cruising in that Vette up the Pike under that giant Exxon sign in the wee, wee hours, thinking up song ideas while listening to his favorite tunes in that bad-ass Corvette.

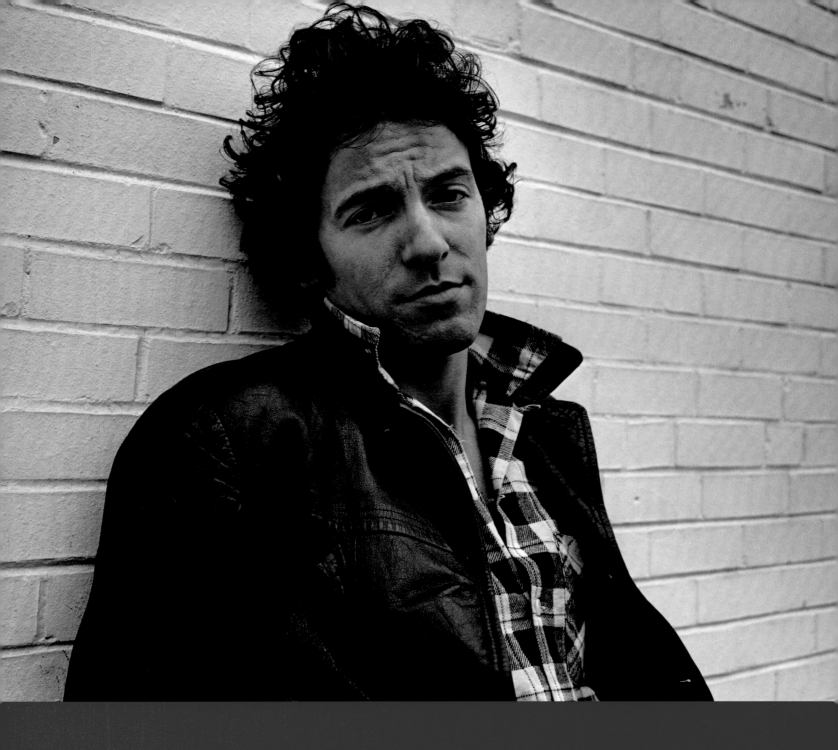

Bruce is a fabulous subject; he has lots of different facets, and he's very animated. In the shot of him against the brick wall, I discovered another facet of Bruce: his acting ability. We were walking through the streets of Haddonfield. It was cold, and we passed this brick wall. I suggested that he just go over and lean against the wall. Bruce seemed to blend right in with the wall, and he gave this look that just melted me. I snapped the photo, and I screamed, "Great!"

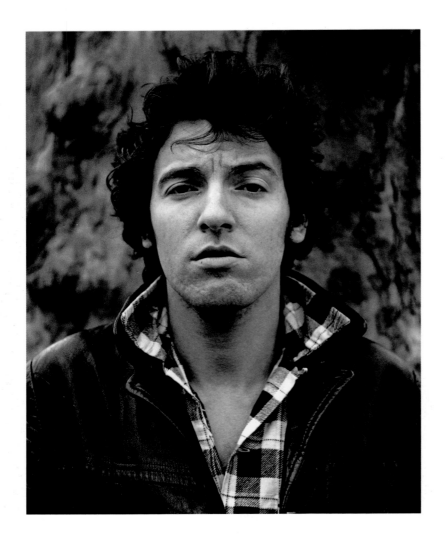

In *Darkness on the Edge of Town*, Bruce was addressing important issues regarding the working class, the family man, and the internal struggle of the individual. It was a very meaningful album for him. He wanted every part to be done right, from the lyrics and the studio recording to the production of the album package. He was also very interested in the photographic process, so he asked if he could come up into the darkroom and see the prints actually being made. In the house, I had a finished but undecorated attic that I turned into a temporary studio and darkroom. There were doors laid across carpenter's sawhorses that I used as tables for the equipment and black material that I used to hang on the wall as backdrops for photographs. I made a kind of tent area that basically served as a portable darkroom for my Besseler enlarger and mixed chemicals. I developed the film from our session on the spot; I put a 6 x 7 centimeter, medium format, black-and-white negative in the enlarger and projected onto 16 x 20-inch fiber paper. As I slid the paper into a tray of developer, Bruce was looking right over my shoulder, watching and waiting. All of a sudden, an image of him materialized.

Bruce hit me on the shoulder, "Frank, that's magic."
"That's not magic. That's darkroom chemistry," I replied.
"No. That's magic."

We had some intense viewing meetings. When the first contact sheets were done of our 1978 Haddonfield session, I drove my car up to Manhattan. There was a snowstorm in New York and New Jersey, so I left the car in lower Manhattan and took a cab up to midtown where Bruce was staying. I brought all the contact sheets up and Bruce said, "Good, let's look at them." We spread them all over the place—on the floor, wherever—and suddenly, Bruce produced a flashlight loupe (a magnifying device). I thought, "Well, this guy knows how to get right into something." He started really looking at each frame. We sat there and critiqued the whole pile of contact sheets. He wanted to know, could I move this over or make something else a little darker? He got very involved in the technicality of the graphics and the photography. Then I would go back to the darkroom, reprint the images, and present them to Bruce again.

Bruce enjoyed observing the process of my work, and I enjoyed watching him get so engrossed in his music. Walking down the street, he would casually notice an unusual sign or billboard, repeat the ad or slogan, and maybe laugh at it. But, having watched him work, it was clear to me that he was processing the words and filing away some esoteric thought in his memory for some future use. I was amazed at how artistic and acutely aware of his surroundings he was and how totally involved he became, not only with writing great songs and playing them, but also with every facet of the packaging of his art. Bruce lives through every part of what he produces, whether it's his own lyrics and music or the graphics and text designed for his album or CD. It's all part of who he is.

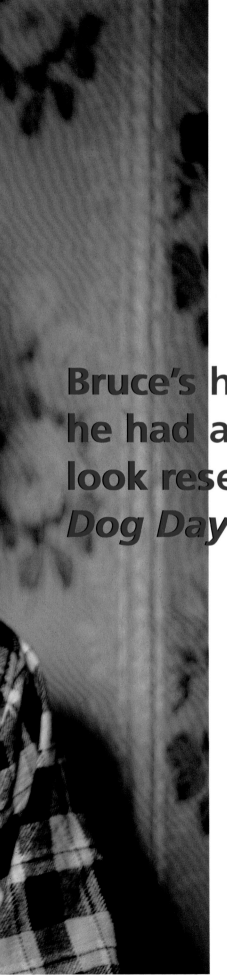

The image ultimately used on the cover of *Darkness on the Edge of Town* was taken in my bedroom in Haddonfield. Bruce picked it from some of the first test pictures that we shot that first day. It was a straightforward shot that evoked a feeling he thought was right for the album. We actually had a couple of different versions of that scene. We used the one of Bruce wearing a leather jacket over a T-shirt on the front cover, and one of him in just the T-shirt on the back cover. Bruce's hair was tousled, and he had a bit of a beard. The look resembled Al Pacino's in *Dog Day Afternoon*. He had been driving back and forth from North Jersey to Haddonfield and running around trying to get the album finalized.

Bruce's hair was tousled, and he had a bit of a beard. The look resembled Al Pacino's in *Dog Day Afternoon.*

EAST CAMDEN, NEW JERSEY, 1978

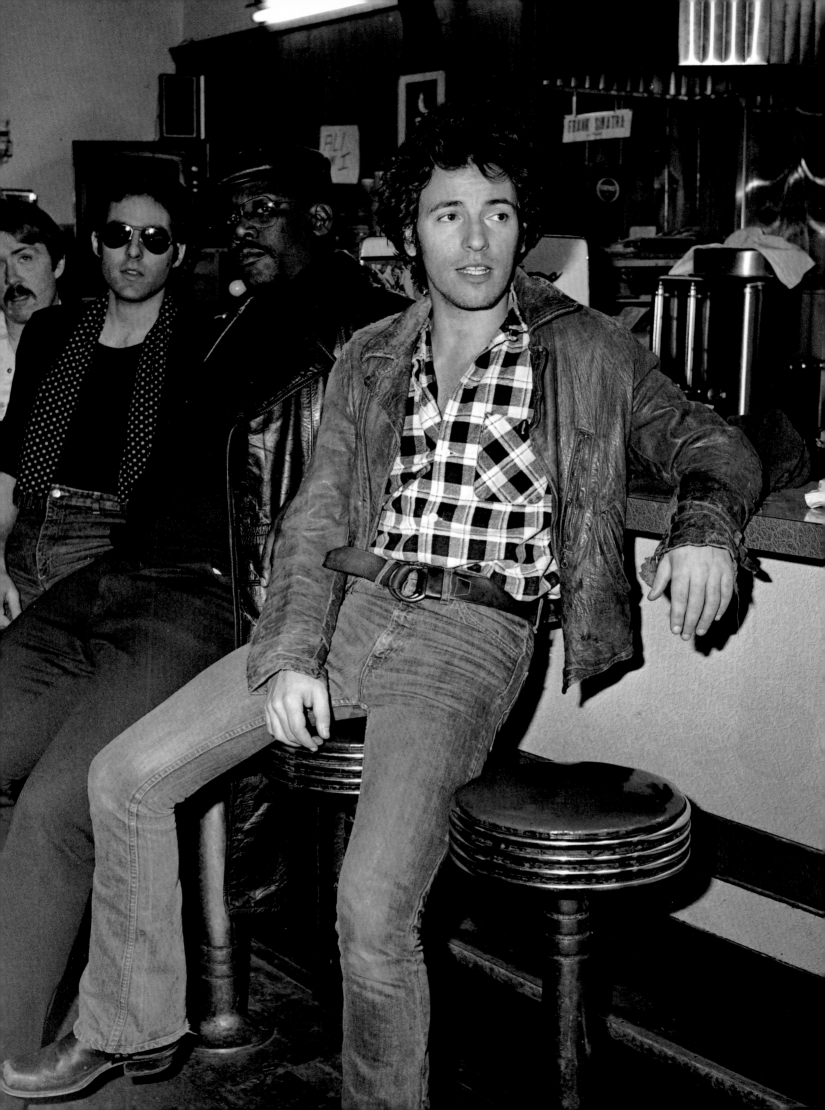

A week after his first visit, Bruce came back to my house with the E Street Band. To have the entire band walk into my living room was pretty amazing. Imagine being in your modest home one minute surrounded by your family, then looking around your living room the next minute and Steve Van Zandt is sitting on your sofa, Bruce Springsteen is standing in the doorway cracking jokes to keep everybody loose, Clarence Clemons is beating your butt playing chess on your coffee table, and the rest of the band is relaxing during the break in shooting. I was thinking to myself as it happened, "Is this my living room or rock and roll heaven?"

To have the band walk into my living room was amazing . . . Imagine looking around and Steve Van Zandt is sitting on your sofa, Bruce is in the doorway cracking jokes.

After we finished shooting at my house, we actually got out in the neighborhood. A music enthusiast and friend of mine, Bill Shellow, a.k.a. Mr. Music, owned a luncheonette called Shellow's Luncheonette that's been around since the late forties/early fifties, in an area called East Camden. There's nothing like Formica and chrome. Throw in a little knotty pine and you're home, baby.

I called Bill up and said, "Stay open. I'm coming over with Bruce Springsteen and the E Street Band."
"Sure you are, Frank."
"No, I really am."

Well, he finally believed me. Bill closed the place for the day, and we invaded the small, old-fashioned luncheonette. We took amazing photographs while Bill cooked cheese steaks for everybody.

All these great musicians are just regular guys. When Max Weinberg, Steven Van Zandt, Clarence Clemons, Roy Bittan, Danny Federici, and Garry Tallent come together on stage, they work as a tight, single-minded unit, but when they're just being themselves, they're distinct, diverse personalities with their own sets of interests. Bruce picked up a lot of these guys when he was in his late teens or early twenties. Look at the photograph of the band from his second album *The Wild, the Innocent & the E Street Shuffle*, whose back cover shot at the beach house was taken by David Gahr. They look exactly like who they are—guys that have been with Bruce for years, from Asbury Park to barefoot on the beach. They and their music grew up together over the years.

Bruce is by far the leader, the instigator, and the storyteller of this group. Sometimes you have a group of guys sitting around waiting for the studio to open up for a set, or in between takes, or on a train or a bus going to a gig, and somebody's got to say something interesting to keep everyone from getting bored. Bruce loved telling wild and outrageous stories with bizarre endings. Sometimes you would get sucked into them only to realize he was having a big joke with you. But sometimes the stories were true; you never knew which was which. Bruce and Steve Van Zandt played off each other all the time, and they could crack each other up. The two are longtime friends with an unspoken understanding between them about what's funny and what's not.

Bruce loved pinball, and there was a terrific pinball machine at Shellow's Luncheonette. In this photo, Stevie's watching him to see how he's going to do. Bruce is very focused on the game. Later that year, I would have the honor of playing pinball with Bruce in a big pinball-machine parlor in Times Square before it was renovated to be so swanky. We were just killing time between shoots in New York City, but he gave the game all his energy. I learned that whether he's picking a guitar, writing a song, performing, helping a friend, or playing pinball, Bruce never does anything halfway.

NEW YORK CITY, NEW YORK, 1978

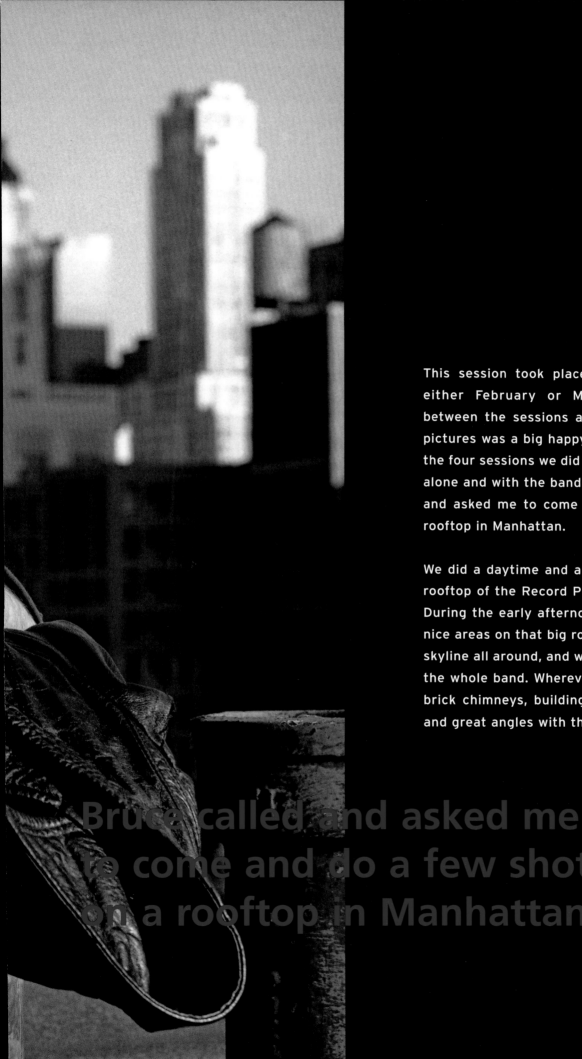

This session took place several weeks later, in either February or March. That whole time between the sessions and the processing of the pictures was a big happy blur. We had already put the four sessions we did in Haddonfield with Bruce alone and with the band to bed when Bruce called and asked me to come and do a few shots on a rooftop in Manhattan.

We did a daytime and a nighttime session on the rooftop of the Record Plant on West 44th Street. During the early afternoon, we found some really nice areas on that big roof with the New York City skyline all around, and we took some pictures with the whole band. Wherever you turned, there were brick chimneys, buildings with tar-covered roofs, and great angles with the city in the background.

Bruce called and asked me to come and do a few shots on a rooftop in Manhattan.

In the late afternoon, my assistants Billy and Benny and Bruce and I took a break and went down to Times Square to play some pinball. Afterwards, we had dinner at a steakhouse and waited for the sun to drop over the horizon. The whole band got back up on the roof, and I took some night shots of the city streets and alleys, which came out beautifully. But taking them was quite tricky. It was so dark up there that we had to illuminate everything with strobes, spots, and hand-held flashlights to get a good focus on the subjects.

After the rooftop session, I scoped out different parts of the office building the same way I did for the session in my house in Haddonfield, trying to find a few interesting angles and areas in which to compose a photograph. We took some corridor shots in the building as well.

Once the whole session was over and the band was packing up to go home, Bruce went into the studio alone and asked me to join him. He sat at the piano and played the most unbelievably soulful version of Elvis Presley's "Heartbreak Hotel" I had ever heard. It was just Bruce and the piano. I felt very privileged to be the only one in the actual sound studio with him.

Bruce admired the music and style of Elvis very much. He told stories about going down to Graceland and trying to get in to see Elvis. Some of the moves that he does on stage, especially those knee jerks, are just like Elvis's. He doesn't do that as much now as he did in the late seventies. Bruce respected the fact that Elvis, with his dungarees, white T-shirt, and leather jacket, was an original, great rock and roll artist who was in synch with his time. Bruce was right for 1978-82 and is still right today.

PHILADELPHIA, PENNSYLVANIA, 1978–
NEW YORK CITY, NEW YORK, 1980

Bruce explodes on stage . . . he maintains a constant energy that touches everybody.

I took these pictures of Bruce and the E Street Band during the *Darkness on the Edge of Town* tour. Although I wasn't really scheduled to shoot at the Spectrum in Philadelphia, in those days you were allowed to bring cameras into a concert and nobody really said anything. I brought my camera and took some pictures from my seat. Even though Bruce didn't authorize it, I couldn't resist capturing parts of the performance on film. Watching those guys operate on stage is incredible.

Before a concert, Bruce is sprawled out on a sofa just being Bruce, quiet and reserved while he takes things in. Then, like a bolt of lightning, he explodes on stage. For an entire three-and-a-half-hour show, he maintains a constant energy that touches everybody in that theater. He is the show. He emits this tremendous amount of energy that just grabs hold of the person sitting way up in a nose-bleeder seat on the other side of the stadium.

The concert at the Spectrum was a great show. Because I had seen many of the performances, I knew the choreography of some of the routines. I had some understanding of how Bruce and the band moved on stage, so I was able to snap at just the right moment, when I knew Bruce was going to either jump up, make a move, or turn.

After working with Bruce on the photos for *Darkness*, he went on tour, and I had the opportunity to work on other projects. In 1979, I shot the front and back covers for *Hearts of Stone*, an album that Steven Van Zandt was producing for Southside Johnny and the Asbury Jukes. I was backstage at a Springsteen concert, and Steven asked me if I would come up to Little Italy in Manhattan the following weekend to do some pictures of Southside Johnny's band. I agreed, and we took over Mulberry and Hester Streets for the whole day, from about eleven o'clock in the morning until eleven o'clock at night. We made friends with everybody in Little Italy that night. I took pictures of the band in different restaurants. The album's front cover shot was taken in front of Puglia's Restaurant on Hester Street, and the back cover shot at Umberto's Clam Bar, which used to be on Mulberry Street. I think they were fascinated with that spot because that's where Crazy Joe Gallo got assassinated. That's a whole other story in itself.

During that time, I also worked with Patti Smith on her album *Radio Ethiopia*. Although none of the photographs I took ever appeared on the album, we did get some really beautiful shots out of that session.

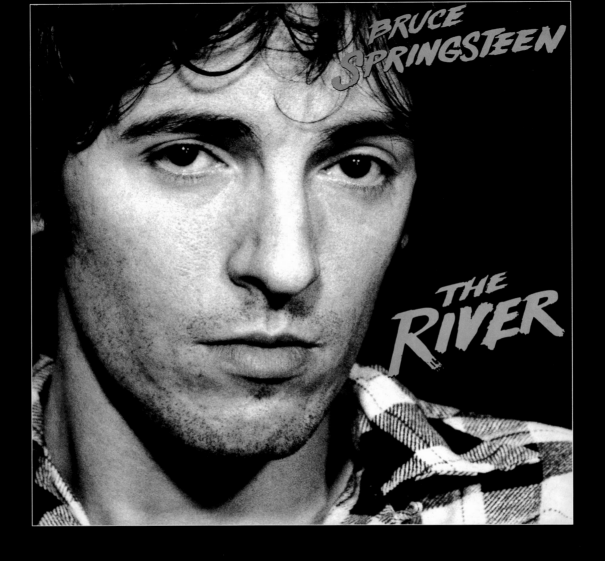

Then, in 1980, Bruce contacted me and said, "We want to take some of the pictures from the *Darkness on the Edge of Town* shoot and use them for *The River*." He had been thinking about this for two years. I'm very grateful that Bruce felt the images we created in that early session were worthy enough to use for two albums.

Getting the cover shot involved a tremendous amount of back-and-forth over the phone. Bruce was out in California mixing *The River*. We each had a set of contact sheets, and three thousand miles apart, we would go over them together at two o'clock in the morning. He would give me directions and ask me if I could do this or that to

We went back and forth until the cover for *The River* emerged—an extreme close-up in black and white . . . Just Bruce looking back at you with the sharp eyes of truth.

a certain picture. Then I would go into the darkroom for an all-night printing session and overnight everything to him in California the next day so he could evaluate it. We went back and forth like this for about two weeks until the cover for *The River* finally emerged. During those long-distance sessions over the phone preparing for *The River*, Bruce told me that he and Jimmy Wachtel, the art director at that time, had the photographs I sent all over the workroom. I imagine they just kept going over them and over them until they had the shot they thought was *The River*—an extreme close-up in black and white with no cover-up. Just Bruce looking back at you with the sharp eyes of truth.

After the album was released and Bruce went on tour, I was given some tickets to see him perform at Madison Square Garden. Years earlier, I had been giving away photographs of mine in the Chelsea Hotel on West Twenty-third Street in Manhattan, just trying to get some recognition. My artist friends who lived down in SoHo witnessed me running around, taking pictures of them, and taking pictures all around the city. When I got a half dozen tickets to see Bruce at Madison Square Garden, I invited all of my New York friends to go with me.

We all jumped in a cab, and when we got to the Garden, my friend Zamba said, "Frank! Look, look!" The whole façade of a building was plastered with a poster of *The River*'s cover image of Bruce's face. I managed to get one of those gigantic cover posters from Columbia Records, and I still have it. There must have been a hundred of them all over the side of the building, and Zamba said, "Frank, you were once giving away pictures at the Chelsea Hotel and now your work is plastered all over Manhattan." It was nice to get that kind of recognition.

HADDONFIELD, NEW JERSEY, 1982

Bruce came back to Haddonfield in 1982 to do a shoot for the upcoming *Nebraska* album. I was still living there with my wife and children. By now, he was making a little more money and could have driven whatever kind of car he wanted, but he went out and bought himself a brand-new midnight blue Camero Z28, and he rumbled up to my house in it on an extremely hot Memorial Day weekend. This was before central air-conditioning for me. I think I only had one air conditioner in the bedroom. We tried shooting inside the house, but the heat was ungodly, so we took pictures outside in the backyard and around the neighborhood.

Since Bruce had become more famous, I had sworn my children, Keith and Lee, to secrecy. "Don't ever tell any of your friends that Bruce Springsteen is in our house working with me," I told them. We didn't want to be interrupted. While we were working in my living room, I had the front window open, and Bruce was changing his shirt for a different look in one of the shots. He said, "Frank, maybe you'd better close your blinds." We looked outside, and there were two carloads of girls in front of my house trying to see Bruce. One of my children had let the cat out of the bag. Bruce was nice enough to autograph a whole bunch of pictures and give them to everybody before sending them on their way.

At that point we decided to leave the area for a while. We were kind of weary from working all morning, so I suggested we take a ride and look for a photo-op out in the field or out on the road somewhere. I had some cassettes in the car, but they were all Bruce Springsteen albums. I didn't want to be embarrassed by playing Bruce his own music, so I asked him to bring a cassette. We jumped into my car and drove out into the New Jersey Pine Barrens. Pine needles were baking on the ground in the sun, and the smell of pine permeated the air. With the windows down and the hot, fragrant air blowing in, I thought of a line from the Springsteen song "Thunder Road": "Roll down the windows and let the wind blow back your hair." Going through back roads down into the swamps of Jersey, Bruce chose to listen to Creedence Clearwater Revival.

Imagine working with the person that you admire the most in rock and roll and having the opportunity to ride through the Jersey Pine Barrens with him with the windows down, playing Creedence Clearwater Revival.

Imagine working with the person that you admire the most in rock and roll, and having the opportunity to take a ride through the Jersey Pine Barrens in the summer with the windows down playing Creedence Clearwater Revival. I can't sing for the life of me, but I harmonized "Lodi" along with Bruce Springsteen in my car. That was one of the greatest days of my life.

We returned to the house to keep working because a fog had rolled in and we wanted to get some shots in it. Sheila had made dinner, so we stopped to join her and the kids at the table. During dinner, we kept hearing a thumping sound under the table, a beat that kept going on and on and on. Since the kids were quite hyperactive and had been drinking a lot of Pepsi, Sheila let out a "Stop doing that!" To her embarrassment, Bruce replied, "Oh, I'm sorry Sheila." He was thinking of a tune.

We worked late that night and Bruce agreed to stay over rather than drive home tired. The next morning I tried, unsuccessfully, to wake him up early because the fog was still out there and I thought we'd get out to take some pictures. He eventually came down later, and we sat out on my front porch. It was still very warm and quiet; the town hadn't woken up yet. My kids, who were in Little League, were out playing ball in the street. I had an old metal glider on the front porch. Bruce and I sat in it, waking up and watching the kids play catch.

Sheila came out and asked him if he wanted some breakfast and he replied, "No, I just want some cookies." We sat in the steamy heat of a quiet morning eating Chips Ahoy cookies and drinking cold milk out on my front porch, when Bruce turned to me and said, "Frank."

"What, Bruce?" I replied.
"You sure are lucky."
"Why am I lucky?"
"Well, you've got this here front porch. I think if I had a front porch like this I'd just sit on it all day long."

It was the most sincere form of saying, "This is nice. You should be thankful for what you have."

It wasn't long after that Bruce bought his first home. I believe it had a front porch.

MONMOUTH COUNTY, NEW JERSEY, 1982

Bruce had been working on a very personal project: an album called *Nebraska*. He still wasn't where he wanted to be with it, so he invited me to a carriage house he was renting on the Navesink River in Monmouth County, New Jersey to do some additional photographs for the project. Although they were never used for *Nebraska*, we did use them in music books accompanying the album, posters, and some other things.

When Bruce called me up to Monmouth, I brought my cameras and all of my equipment. I walked around the carriage house a little bit and looked out on the river to take in the atmosphere of the location. We went up to the room he was using as a bedroom, and I sat down in this big easy chair. To give me the true feeling of *Nebraska*, he played a cassette recording of the album. He had recorded it on a four-track tape-recording machine and was planning to clean it up in the studio. Ultimately, they went back to this original four-track recording for the final release.

I sat down alone with Bruce and he showed me a Snoopy binder in which he had written all the lyrics for his new album. Before it was released, I read the original lyrics to all the great songs in *Nebraska* in ballpoint pen while the entire album was playing and Bruce was sitting across from me. It was a wonderful experience. This was true heartland music. He had been reading a lot of Woody Guthrie at the time, as well as a lot about the Charles Starkweather murder rampage, about which he wrote in one of the songs on *Nebraska*. He wrote about America—the regular guy, the working guy, the family guy, and the hardships of being a middle-class American. Like Dylan, Springsteen is a powerful poet writing tremendously important songs about our times. Some of the songs were reflective and some whimsical, but all constituted very strong poetry for the people, and I think John Hammond of Columbia Records, who signed both of them, recognized that. In some of Bruce's early work, like *Nebraska*, the poetry was fluid and the guitar-work was quick and precise.

When the cassette was finished, Bruce very quietly turned off the tape recorder and asked, "What do you think?" All I could say was "Wow! The only thing I can tell you is that if I can get my pictures to be half as good as the pictures that you're creating with words, then I will have done my job." David Michael Kennedy's power-ful windshield photo on the cover of *Nebraska* projected the rawness I believe Bruce was looking for—a stark atmosphere that parodied the starkness of the charac-ters he writes about on the album. I think Bruce had a good idea of what he wanted the look of that cover image to be, and David nailed it.

We had dinner together that night after the *Nebraska* session. Sitting on the deck of his house, Bruce told me a story about his nephew's confirmation party. He said he had watched his nephew run across the lawn with his confirmation gown trailing behind him, and he said that as he watched, "all I could see was lost youth. Lost youth." That theme evolved into a song called "Glory Days," which appears on his album *Born in the U.S.A.*

Springsteen's lyrics are visual and evocative—the song "Mansion on the Hill" is a good example. Bruce mentioned to me several times that not all images depicted in words need to be portrayed graphically. Every person who listens to "Mansion on the Hill" conjures up something different. Everyone has his or her own idea of what that mansion looks like. When Bruce and I did concentrate on images, they had to be equally evocative. Once, we did a sequence at Hopkins Pond in the woods in Haddonfield. Those woods were not thick or ominously dark, but Bruce told me that the woods should seem thick, dark, and scary the way he saw them. He had very definite ideas about using a composition of words to create a mental image, and then selecting the

Bruce was very proud of his Gibson steel-string acoustic guitar . . . He wanted to use it in some of the shots.

Bruce was very proud of the guitar in these photos. It was a Gibson steel-string acoustic guitar. I remember him showing it to me. He very, very carefully opened up the guitar case. It was sitting in there shining, and he said, "What do you think of that?" He wanted to use it in some of the shots, so strumming it was just a natural thing. It was there; why not play it and perhaps hum a few tunes while playing? Doing that made him comfortable while we set up the composition of the shot.

By 1982, Bruce had become much more popular and his concerts were selling out, but he was always comfortable to work with and had a great sense of humor. We always had time to joke, laugh, and talk about life in general, but I couldn't quite look at him the same way as I did in 1978. I was a little more in awe. He was certainly much more the star in 1982 than he was when we first started working together in 1978.

AFTERWORD

One thing about the group of artists in New York that I knew in the late '70s and early '80s, especially among the Jersey kids like myself, Patti Smith, Bruce Springsteen, and Southside Johnny Lyons, was that everybody helped each other as much as they could. Perhaps some day one of us would create a poem, a record, or a photograph that would make it, and we would have the chance to prove ourselves to the world. We all had hope and dreams.

Just imagine being able to pick your favorite movie star or your favorite rock musician and work with that person. Photography was the one constant in my life. Since the age of eight, and through several different jobs, I continually took photographs. I loved photography. I loved composing the picture and seeing the print emerge. To have the opportunity to photograph the one artist that I most admired and to whom I related the most was nothing short of magic to me. The sincerest form of flattery was to know that Bruce, a master very much in control of himself and his art, gave me the freedom to portray him the way I saw him, and he considered that work to be worthy.

I'm very big on the Rolling Stones, Bob Dylan, David Bowie, and the other artists that I grew up with, but when I heard Bruce Springsteen's music, that was it. For me, his music tied it all together. I felt as if he invented the music for me—not just because of the Jersey connection, but because of the way he was talking, the feelings that he was evoking, and the lifestyle that he was leading. While working with him, I discovered that Bruce is just a reg-ular guy trying to tell his story and speak up for the guy that can't speak up for himself. He wants his music to make people see and notice something they may not have even looked at or noticed otherwise.

Bruce remains strong in his commitment to his subject matter. He hasn't sold out in terms of what he's writing or singing about. He's maintained everything through honesty—honesty in the music, honesty about his sense of self-worth, and honesty in his dealings with people. Bruce Springsteen has upheld a very strong sense of what he's about, and you can see that in the way he works with people and in his work.

Integrity defines Bruce in every sense of the word. He's straight up and hasn't been swayed by the forces of evil. He's very wise and knows how to pace himself. Fortunately, he has elevated himself to a stature in the music business that is so strong he doesn't have to be anybody's puppet; no one is pulling his strings. A lot of my admiration for Bruce comes from a respect for his intelligence and the strength and integrity of his work. Because he keeps it real, Bruce Springsteen and the E Street Band are still together and touring three decades after these photos were taken.

All in all, working with Bruce has been more than just a photographic trip. I'm still a fan. I was Bruce's photographer in the early years, and others have been since. But I've never stopped being a fan. Springsteen keeps it real. That's the deal. He keeps it real and doesn't go in for the glitz and glitter of showbiz. He goes in for the true art. That's what he does.

When I started working with Bruce in 1978, I knew I was in the presence of something great. I told Patti Smith that I thought Bruce would be famous, but at that time, I don't think anyone, with the possible exception of Bruce himself, could have foreseen the magnitude of how this man, his music, his band, his presence, and his amazingly prolific and sensitive artistry would evolve.

Bruce Frederick Springsteen casts a long shadow. He's one of a kind, an original legend. I have often said, "It's not what you take with you in this life, it's what you leave behind." Bruce is leaving behind a legacy of wonderful songs, great music, unbelievable stage shows, a strong family circle, loyal friends, and a commitment to humanity and the planet. Thanks to the opportunity I had to work with Bruce during those days of hope and dreams, I can leave behind these photographs and anecdotes for you to enjoy.

ACKNOWLEDGMENTS

My thanks to: my inspiration, Carol Reed, who traveled across time and space to bring hope and dreams. Lee and Keith Stefanko for never giving up on the old man. Mom and Dad for teaching the value of hard work and miracles. Steve Stefanko for all the support a true brother can give. Chris Murray at Govinda Gallery for embracing and orchestrating the project. Carol Huh and Kate Adjemian at Govinda Gallery. Patti Smith, artist, poet, mystic, and friend—without you these photographs would never have been. Colleen Sheehy of the Frederick Weisman Art Museum for her insight and her foresight. Bob Santelli of the Experience Music Project for your encouragement. Sandra and Harry Choron for many years of help and support. Billy and Gail Silverman, true friends through thick and thin. Mick Rock who gave me the great speech about getting off my butt and sharing these photographs. Master Printer Bobby Geist, Jim Eby, Mike Leddy, Joe Thompson, III, Allison, and the entire crew at Berry & Homer, in Philadelphia. Raoul and Gordon Goff at Palace Press for their creative energy, and Bob Nirkind and Elizabeth Wright at Watson-Guptill Publications. Debra Minter for her technical advice and constant support. Frank Montemurro for Frank's Barbershop, a classic. Dan Reed and Suzy Freeman for their help and opinion in choosing images. Gloria Goldenberg, my sister, whose spirit is always with me. Teri Corrigan for believing it could be done. Ken Tisa, the best artist I know and dear friend who, twenty-five years ago, said, "Don't ever lose those negatives." Benedict and Stacy Tisa for their support, hospitality, and enthusiasm. Dave Marsh for your help and encouragement. Everyone at Jon Landau Management, including Tammy McGurk, Sue Berger, and especially Barbara Carr and Jon Landau. Special thanks to Steve Van Zandt, Garry Tallent, Max Weinberg, Clarence Clemons, Roy Bittan, Danny Frederici, Ms. Patti Scialfa. Mr. Bruce Frederick Springsteen.
—Frank Stefanko

Thank you to Virginia for sending Frank my way. To Bruce for his Rock & Roll spirit. And to Frank for sharing his heart and soul with me.

—Chris Murray

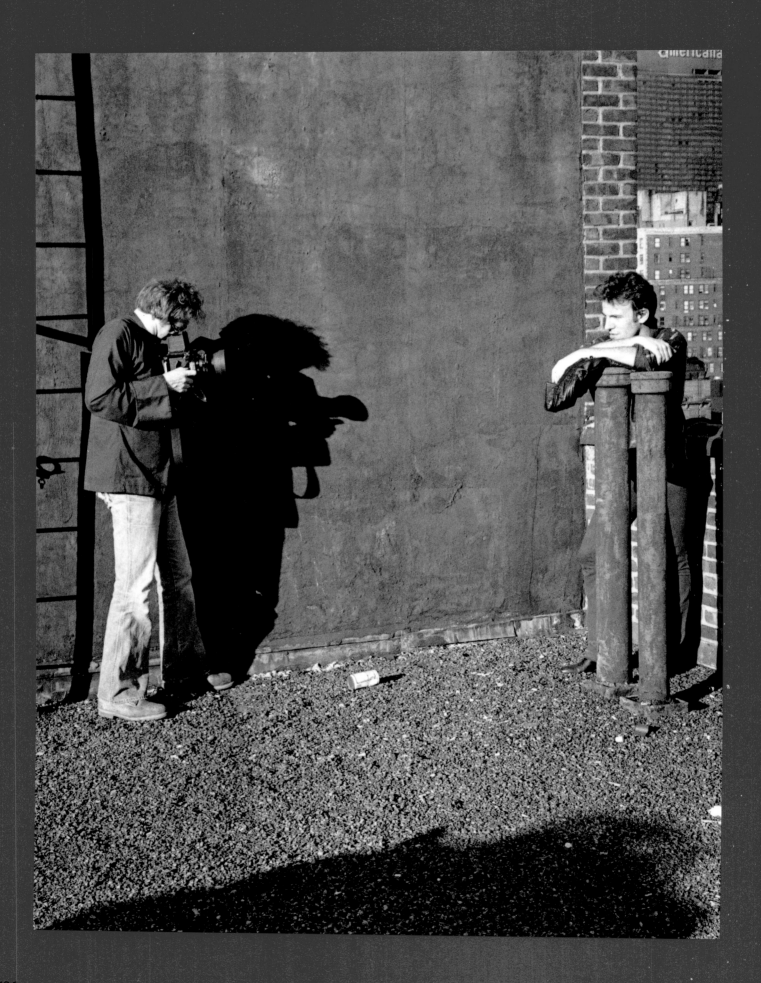